SANDRA AND WILLIAM MARKLE

GONE FOREVER!

AN ALPHABET OF EXTINCT ANIMALS

ILLUSTRATED BY FELIPE DÁVALOS

SCHOLASTIC INC.
New York Toronto London Auckland Sydney
Mexico City New Delhi Hong Kong

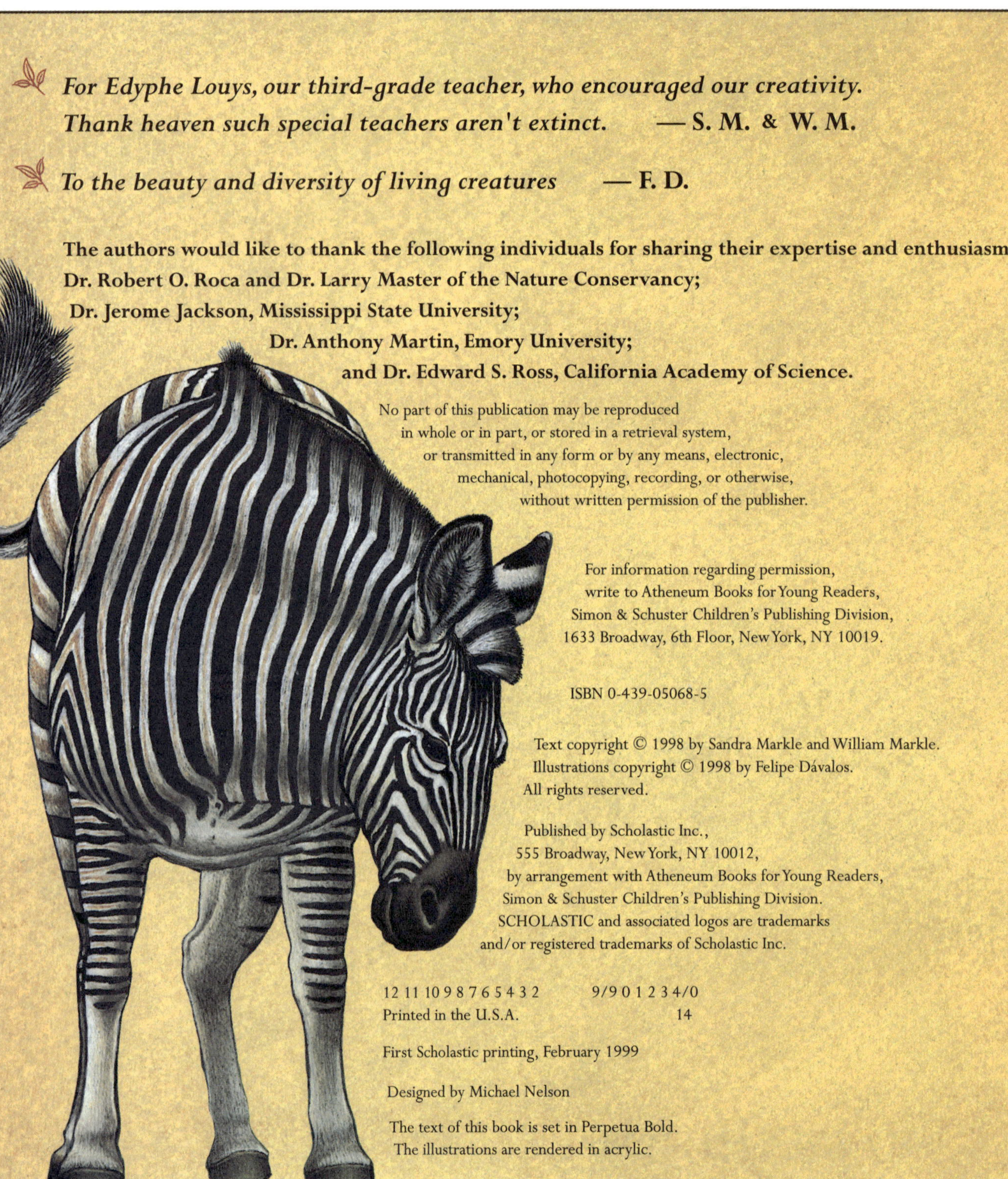

For Edyphe Louys, our third-grade teacher, who encouraged our creativity. Thank heaven such special teachers aren't extinct. — **S. M. & W. M.**

To the beauty and diversity of living creatures — **F. D.**

The authors would like to thank the following individuals for sharing their expertise and enthusiasm: Dr. Robert O. Roca and Dr. Larry Master of the Nature Conservancy; Dr. Jerome Jackson, Mississippi State University; Dr. Anthony Martin, Emory University; and Dr. Edward S. Ross, California Academy of Science.

For information regarding permission, write to Atheneum Books for Young Readers, Simon & Schuster Children's Publishing Division, 1633 Broadway, 6th Floor, New York, NY 10019.

ISBN 0-439-05068-5

Published by Scholastic Inc., 555 Broadway, New York, NY 10012, by arrangement with Atheneum Books for Young Readers, Simon & Schuster Children's Publishing Division.
SCHOLASTIC and associated logos are trademarks and/or registered trademarks of Scholastic Inc.

12 11 10 9 8 7 6 5 4 3 2 9/9 0 1 2 3 4/0
Printed in the U.S.A. 14

First Scholastic printing, February 1999

Designed by Michael Nelson

The text of this book is set in Perpetua Bold.
The illustrations are rendered in acrylic.

You know there were once dinosaurs on Earth and that they are now gone. When there are no more of an animal, it's said to be extinct. This book is about animals that lived much more recently than dinosaurs. Some only became extinct while your grandparents or parents were children. But once an animal is gone, there is no way to bring it back.

Auroch

Imagine cave paintings of these wild oxen come to life! It's no mistake that the ancient artists made them look huge. Aurochs (ôr′-oks) were nearly as big as elephants and had splendid long horns. They were the great-grandparents of today's cattle.

Once, large herds roamed over what is now Europe and Asia. But they were hunted for food and to make trophies of their horns. When only a few were left, the aurochs were protected by guards. But hunters managed to raid this herd, too. The last auroch died in 1627, leaving only the cave paintings as memories.

Aa

Atlas Bear

Hunters didn't cause the Atlas Bear to disappear—it was the desert. Remains that have been found show that these bears once roamed over all of North Africa. That was when this region was covered by forests rich in fruits and nuts. Farmers wanting to plant crops and builders needing timber cut down trees. Over time, the soil blew away and the land became a desert. After that, Atlas Bears only lived in the forested Atlas Mountains of Morocco and in zoos. By the late 1800s, these bears were gone, too.

Bb

Before World War I, catching these fish was big business on Lakes Michigan and Huron in North America. In summertime, fishermen in boats hauled in nets bulging with ciscos. In winter, fishermen huddled in shacks tugged the glistening ciscos through holes cut in the ice. After many years of such heavy fishing, few ciscos remained and most of the fishermen quit.

Over time, the number of ciscos would have increased, but by then sea lampreys had entered the lakes. These eel-like animals probably killed the last ciscos. Not one of these fish has been seen since 1960.

Blackfin Cisco and Deepwater Cisco

Cc

Dd

Dodo Bird

What a funny-looking bird! Fat and nearly as big as today's turkeys, its wings were too tiny for flight. Of course, since it lived on an island and had no enemies, the dodo did not need to fly.

Then, in the late 1500s, settlers arrived on Mauritius and Reunion islands off the southeast coast of Africa, the dodo's homeland. They found the odd birds tasty and easy to catch. Rats from the ships ate the birds' eggs. In less than a hundred years, all of the dodos were gone. When this news reached Europe, people were shocked that it was possible to wipe out an entire group of animals so quickly.

Dodo Tree

Is it possible that some plants need animals to survive? For years, people believed no new dodo trees could sprout. This tree's fruit has an extra-thick seed coat which was thought to break down only as it passed through the dodo's digestive system. Today, scientists think Mauritius Island's extinct parrots and fruit-eating bats may have been just as important to its dodo trees as the dodos. Of the few dodo tree saplings that still sprout each year, very few survive. The saplings have to compete with plants people introduced to the island. Pigs and deer also eat the young saplings. So for many reasons, the dodo tree may one day become extinct just like the dodo.

Elephant Bird

Imagine an egg so big that the empty shell could hold two gallons of milk! That's how big the elephant bird's eggs were. The elephant bird was a giant about three meters (almost ten feet) tall—much taller than the tallest basketball player. Ancient hunters probably killed the elephant bird for food and ate its eggs. But it may have become extinct because the climate changed. Elephant bird remains have been found mainly in what was once wet, swampy land on Madagascar, an island off Africa, but today, those swamps are dry land.

Ff

This frog's swampy home dried up too, but not because of a change in the weather. In the late 1940s, the Israelis drained the area around Hula Lake just north of the Sea of Galilee so that people could build homes. But that swampland was the home of the Palestinian painted frog. No longer than a half stick of butter, this little frog spent its days safely burrowed into the sandy swamp bottom with just its head sticking out of the water. At night, it came out to hunt for bugs. Always rare, none have been seen since 1955.

Palestinian Painted Frog

Great Auk

Does the great auk remind you of today's penguins? Unlike penguins, which live mainly in the far south, the great auk lived in the far north. But like penguins, each year great auks came ashore and gathered in large groups to nest. Then people killed the adult auks for food and used their soft feathers to stuff mattresses. They stole their eggs too.

When the great auks became rare in the mid-1800s, museums eager to mount displays offered a reward, and hunters quickly killed off the few auks that remained.

Gg

Heath Hen

Once, springtime in New England was alive with the roar of hundreds of noisy male heath hens attracting mates. But settlers hunted these birds, and farmers chopped down their home forests. By 1830, heath hens could only be found on Martha's Vineyard, an island off the coast of Massachusetts.

There, protected by law, the heath hen population soared to almost two thousand. Then in 1916 a fire during the nesting season killed all but a hundred birds. A hard winter a few years later killed more. Then disease wiped out all but one. That last heath hen died in 1932.

Hh

Portuguese Ibex

A hunter had to be strong and clever to catch a Portuguese ibex (ī´-beks). This wild goat could run along narrow mountain ledges and bound up steep, rocky slopes. But being hard to get only made its beautiful horns a more valuable trophy. Local villagers also hunted the Portuguese ibex for food and to make medicine from the stone-like lumps that form in its stomach.

Once hunters had guns, it became easier to kill these graceful animals. The more guns improved, the rarer the Portuguese ibex became. The last known sighting was in 1892.

Ii

An old Indian might have followed the trail of jaguar footprints to the deer remains the big cat had buried. Native Americans unable to hunt on their own sometimes found food this way. And the Arizona jaguar had no trouble catching more. It was the top hunter in its range, which spread across the forested mountains of eastern Arizona, the southern half of western New Mexico, and southern California. Then settlers moved in and pushed the cat out of its homeland and hunted it for its beautiful skin. The last reported sighting of an Arizona jaguar was in New Mexico in 1905 by the hunters who killed it.

Arizona Jaguar

Jj

Norfolk Island Kaka

What a surprise to hear a dog barking in the treetops! That's what the first settlers of the Norfolk and Phillip islands in the South Pacific thought, until they discovered what made that sound—a colorful parrot called the Norfolk Island kaka. It nested in hollow trees or in holes in the rocks and mainly ate nectar, the sweet liquid made by flowers. Like the dodo, this island bird had never had to stay away from enemies until people arrived, so it was easy to catch. Most of the Norfolk Island kakas were eaten. The only survivors were a few kept as pets. Long after the last wild birds were gone, one lived on in a cage in London until 1851.

L1

Barbary Lion

Barbary lions, which lived in North Africa, were much bigger than today's lions. The male was only a little shorter than some cars and had a dark mane covering nearly half its body. Like the Atlas bear, the lions suffered when the ancient farmers chopped down the trees. With the forest gone, the animals these cats hunted left or died off. Many Barbary lions were caught by the Romans to show at their sports arenas.

Finally, like the Atlas bear, the Barbary lions only survived in the rugged forest of North Africa's Atlas Mountains. But better guns made it easier to hunt even in such wild places. Hunters killed the last Barbary lions in the 1920s.

Moa

Was this what moas really looked like? People think so, but the only clues they have to go on are bones, skin, and feathers. There are also stories that have been passed down by the Maoris, the native people who hunted these flightless birds on New Zealand and nearby islands. No one is sure just when moas became extinct, but the hunting stories date it to about the mid-1800s.

From the remains, scientists believe there were a number of different types of moas—some nearly four meters (twelve feet) tall.

Nn

Oahu Nukupu'u

People know this was a small bird that ate nectar, collecting it from deep inside tube-shaped flowers with its long, curved beak. But that's all anyone knows. The Oahu Nukupu'u (ō-ä´-ho͞o no͞o-ko͞o-po͞o´-o͞o) disappeared from its home island of Oahu in the Hawaiian Islands before anyone had studied it. No one is even sure why it became extinct. Maybe it was because the European settlers brought cattle that trampled the flowering undergrowth. Or maybe it caught a disease from the birds the settlers brought to the island. Whatever happened, all of the Oahu Nukupu'u were gone by the 1890s.

Oo

Syrian Onager

Carvings on the walls at Nineveh, the capital city of ancient Assyria, show hunters lassoing two onagers (on´-ə-jərs) from a thundering herd. Through the years, the desert people continued to hunt these small wild asses for food. But this didn't shrink the huge herds of onagers that roamed across the Hammad and Nafud deserts. Then, during World War I, armies overran the desert. Many Syrian onagers were shot or struck by trucks. The herds were broken up, and within a few years these animals became scarce. Hunters killed the last wild Syrian onager, but one lived on in a Vienna zoo until 1927.

Passenger Pigeon

Once, passenger pigeons in search of food migrated across North America in flocks so big they blocked out the sun. Nesting colonies often filled all the treetops for miles. So many parents on guard kept the chicks safe from hawks and other animals. But such huge flocks also attracted the birds' worst enemy—human hunters. Thousands of passenger pigeons were shot in a day, to send the meat to market or just for fun. As the flocks shrank, the chicks became easier prey for animal predators. By 1910, only Martha, a female who lived at the Cincinnati Zoo in Ohio, was left. She died September 1, 1914.

Pp

Quagga

Does this look like a zebra missing some of its stripes? The quagga (kwag´-ə) was a close relative of today's zebras. The natives called it *quahkah,* imitating its shrill barking voice. In the 1600s, the Dutch who settled on its home range on Africa's Cape of Good Hope changed the name to quagga. They also rounded up and killed as many of these grazing animals as they could catch. The Dutch wanted to save the grasslands for their own herds of cattle. Because of their exotic striped coats, a few quagga were shipped to European zoos, but no effort was made to breed them there. The last quagga died in the Amsterdam Zoo in 1883.

Qq

Captain Maclear's Rat

Imagine an island swarming with big rats—many longer than a man's foot! That's what an English sea captain named Maclear discovered in 1886. It was on Christmas Island, just 200 miles south of Java in the South Pacific. But these were friendly rats that only ate fruit and tender plant shoots.

The rats lived on undisturbed after the island's discovery. Then in 1906 a mining settlement was established. And within three years, all of Captain Maclear's rats were dead. Some had been killed by the vicious ship's rats that invaded the island. Many more, it's believed, were killed by diseases these new rats brought with them.

Rr

Ss

Steller's Sea Cow

When Georg Wilhem Steller first saw the animals named for him, there were thousands in the icy waters around Bering and Copper islands in the North Pacific off Russia. He thought their rough, dark backs poking out of the water looked like overturned boats. Then several lifted their snouts, snorting mist and chomping seaweed with toothless, bony gums. The sea cows crawling through the shallows were as gentle as they looked. Hunters killed them so easily for their meat and thick fat that they were all gone in less than thirty years from the time they were discovered. The last Steller's sea cow was killed on Bering Island in 1767.

Rodriguez Greater Tortoise

Measure a line a meter (three feet) long and you'll see just how big this tortoise was. In the days of sailing ships, both the French and English navies regularly stopped at Rodriguez Island in the Indian Ocean to pick up these tortoises to eat during long sea voyages.

As the number of tortoises shrank, rules were set up to regulate how many each ship could take, but no one obeyed them. Then several shiploads of tortoises were sent to another island for protection. But so many died on the way that the tortoise population was even smaller than before. By 1795, the Rodriguez greater tortoises were gone forever.

Utah Lake Sculpin

The 1930s were very dry in Utah. The level of Utah Lake dropped lower and lower. This lake was the only home for a kind of fish called the Utah Lake sculpin. As shallow parts of the lake dried up, the sculpin had fewer places to lay its eggs. The small number of young fish that hatched were gobbled up by hungry bigger fish, so few grew up to replace the dying adults. No Utah Lake sculpin has been seen since 1936. This was an animal that became extinct because of bad weather!

Uu

Gull Island Vole

These meadow mice lived only on the Gull Islands off the east coast of Long Island, New York. Like other types of voles, they dug tunnels through the soft, moist soil to find seeds, bulbs, and tender plant shoots to eat. Then, during the Spanish-American War, soldiers dug trenches and built walls all over these islands to prevent possible attack. This destroyed the voles' homes and many died. In 1898, when a researcher came to the island to study the voles, he couldn't find any. None have been seen since.

Tasmanian Wolf

This animal was called a wolf because it hunted other animals and looked a little like a wolf. But it was not a wolf. The female carried her newborn babies in a pouch the way a kangaroo does.

When Europeans settled in Tasmania, an island off Australia, and wild game became scarce, Tasmanian (taz-mā´-nē-ən) wolves began to hunt farm animals. The settlers then hunted the wolves. Too late, people tried to save this animal. In 1966, the government created a game reserve for the Tasmanian wolf in hopes some might still be alive. But none have been seen since the last one died in Tasmania's Hobart Zoo in 1934.

Ww

Xx

Xerces Blue Butterfly

Imagine seeing shimmering blue-violet butterflies fluttering over wildflowers. That was the brilliant color of the male xerces (zerk´-sēz) blue butterfly. The female was brown. Always rare, the xerces butterflies lived only on the San Franciscan Peninsula in California. The cool, foggy summers there seemed to suit them perfectly. Then people built on this land, clearing away the lupine, deerweed, and other wildflowers where the females laid their eggs. When the caterpillars hatched, they couldn't find enough of the food they needed to grow and change into butterflies. The more buildings there were, the rarer these butterflies became. The last adults were collected in 1941. Some can be seen mounted in museums, but their brilliant blue color is now faded.

Cuban Yellow Bat

All that is known about this bat comes from fossil remains found inside a cave near Daiquiri, Cuba. Experts guessed it must be something like its relatives surviving in the Bahamas and in South America. They figured it had slender legs and funnel-shaped ears. But the fossils show it was bigger and more heavily built. It's also a guess to assume that it became extinct in the late 1800s, but the cause was almost certainly a loss of food. The Cuban yellow bat is thought to have been a picky eater, specializing in a certain kind of fruit. When these fruit trees were cleared away, the bats probably starved even if other food was available.

Yy

Zz

Burchell's Zebra

In the mid-1800s, wealthy Englishmen liked to have a pair of these beautiful black-and-white striped zebras pulling their carriages. But the wild herds that roamed the South African grassland weren't appreciated. Once, this animal's main enemy had been the lion. Then farmers moved onto its home range. They killed all the Burchell's zebras they could catch because these animals ate the grass needed by their herds of cattle. The last captive Burchell's zebra died in the London Zoo in 1910, many years after they were gone from the wild.

Now you know about a few of the many animals that are extinct. Sadly, many more are in danger, but you can help protect them. First, look for birds and butterflies and other wild animals living right around you and find out what they need to survive. Be willing to share your neighborhood and its resources with them. Then think about animals living in other parts of the world this same way—as neighbors sharing the earth. Sometimes, a little less for people can keep more animals from becoming gone forever.

Organizations You Can Join to Help Protect Wildlife

Environmental Stewardship Program
National 4-H Council
7100 Connecticut Avenue
Chevy Chase, MD 20815-4999
301-961-2833

Earth Savers Club
National Wildlife Federation
8925 Leesburg Pike
Vienna, VA 22184
800-822-9919

School Yard Habitat Program
National Wildlife Federation
PO Box 9004
Winchester, VA 22604-9004
800-477-5560

Save Our Streams
Adopt a Stream
Isaac Walton League of America
707 Conservation Lane
Gaithersburg, MD 20878
800-284-4952 or 301-548-0150